Blue Fire

A POETIC JOURNEY OF OUR EMOTIONS
VOLUME 1

By Lydia Cook

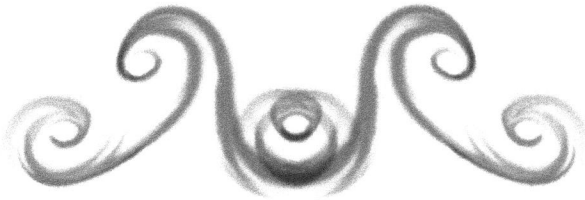

LOVE . HATE
JOY . PAIN . REGRET
FORGIVENESS . STRENGTH . GROWTH

WITHOUT GOD
NOTHING IS POSSIBLE!

ChoiceWordsss – Attention Permissions
PO Box 886
Hendersonville, TN 37077-0886

For information about creative works and book ordering, please contact Lydia Cook of ChoiceWordsss, at: ChoiceWordsss@gmail.com.

All Illustrations, Cover Art, and text is Copyright Protected by My Original Works. Reference #60192.

Ordering Information:
To order additional copies of this book, please visit Amazon, or:
https://www.createspace.com/4715588

ISBN-13: 978-0615989952
ISBN-10: 0615989950

Cover Art, Editing and Formatting by Selina Ahnert of Miyasia. To contact Miyasia, email at: tiger_ki10@yahoo.com.

Second Edition Printing, 2014

Table of Contents

Why I Write

To all those that have been such a big part of my life, my gratitude will forever be present! My hope is that this book touches many lives by empowering, inspiring, and spreading the realistic picture of tests and trials. May I send the Love back out into the world as I've been blessed to receive it from you!

Also, remember; never get so caught up in the chase that you forget about God... because through God, all things are possible.

Sincerely, Lydia...

Our Story, God's Glory!

For years, I looked at life and asked you why?

Why all the suffering, pain, and anguish?

Why, God, Why?

How can you be our Father and permit such actions?

How?

Why, God, Why?

And a voice so clear and still says,

"Do you not Still Love?"

How?

"Because of my Love; that's how!"

"Have I not protected you from Yourself, and others?"

Why?

"Because, I Love you."

"That's why!"

"You and many other of my chosen vessels."

"And even I rested on the 7th day."

Why?

"Because I needed the Rest."

Yes, I still Love,

And when life almost made me bitter,

I chose Love

True!

So many times, it was hard for me to forgive myself and others!

But your agape Love shines through!

Thank you!

But what do I do, now?

I understand the Purpose behind the abuse,

The Victory behind the tears,

The Power behind the Pain!

The Strength behind the regret,

But God, I am but one Soul!

Why have you placed this calling upon me?

This longing to see our world a better place…

The need to see people free...

"There are many people who feel exactly the way you felt!"

"And understand this hurts me, too."

"Yes, I am God, but I have feelings just the same."

"To see men that I created killing, raping, drugging, misleading, and thieving."

"This, too, saddens my omnipresence."

"What you do, my child, is you surround yourself with likeminded chosen vessels."

"You must trust, be open, lead and be led!"

"Utilize your gift of words, your gift of speech, and compel those in discomfort not to lose faith!"

"Share your testimony, freely, as to be a beacon of light and hope."

"Continue to step out of your comfort zone and MOVE FORWARD!"

"And as I have throughout the hands of time… I WILL do the rest!"

OUR STORY, GOD'S GLORY!

Ever Missed You?

…Then she looked around
everyone was smiling, except for her…
The feeling is like the worst crash and burn, ever!
For once,
time came to a complete stop.
All she hears
is her mind
commanding her lungs to breathe!
Some good intensions
lead to a bad direction.
In this moment of honesty,
pain reeked from her soul.
And I realized "her" was me… and I miss me!
The laughing, carefree,
glass half full me…
The beyond a shadow of a doubt me.
The I love everyone
regardless to their race, religion, or sexuality me!
The goof ball
but still trying to be cool me…
I lost her in you,

trying to be all
that you required me to be!
I fell prey to that wounded little girl
she used to be.
For some odd reason,
nothing else in the world mattered but your happiness!
The same comfort you provided led down a path of control.
Then, I looked around;
decided I refuse to live like her.
Because the best part of me
is exactly that, Being Me.

Memory's Pages

Scrolling through the pages
Of my mind!
Thinking of people,
Places and times.
Wondering, what if,
What if…
We could erase the hands of time.
Pour the sand back in the glass,
Trading tears,
For joy and laughs!
On these pages,
There are many faces,
Variations of colors,
Sisters and brothers,
Friends, and partners,
Passionate lovers!
With the turn of each page,
Memories roll through the sky,
Saddened that mistrust,
Allowed me to say goodbye!

Goodbye to kind souls,
Because others treated me cold!
There are some pages that are very bright,
Pages when I lived in the light!
These pages are brand new and exciting,
Like the smell of a new car.
Yes, the days
When I feel like a beautiful star!
Not a star you'd find in Hollywood,
The type that's free in the night,
The kind that owns life,
That star that admires living life right!
Writing new pages,
And beginning new journeys.
My hope is to have
The sweetest joy in the morning!
Scrolling through these pages,
Never know what I'll see.
Only thing I know,
Is there's a different kind of me!

Family Tree

Ever look in the mirror
and wonder whose smile you see,
considering your family tree?
I've often thought,
"why are my eyebrows so thick"?
And if someone in my generation
has the shape of my lips?
Those of you who know your family,
you are truly blessed!
Never had a family reunion
or shared the results of a pregnancy test!
Always wanted a niece
that as I look in her eyes,
I could follow a trail to our elders.
I would fantasize about Sunday dinners, reciting a poem,
and granny says, "that's my baby"!
No, it doesn't sadden my heart
as much as it used to!
On Holidays, my mind still drifts…
Maybe, in the next lifetime,

I'll have four or five sisters,
and we will argue over shoes
and who is the best dresser!
Then, we'd get married,
sharing diaper war stories!
Maybe, fuss about our spouses
and how they get on our nerves.
Then, go to the mall,
and watch our children grow old, together.
Family trees
are a blessing, indeed!

No Longer Blind

Please, don't think my Love is blind,
For my heart will always see!
My ears will forever hear
The lies you turned out to be.
No need for yelling,
No need for shouts.
Save the empty promises
That release from your mouth!
I am not angry, nor am I sad.
Tell you the truth, my spirit is glad!
Glad that it's over,
So new life can begin,
I Love you
Still consider you friend!
But our time has ended;
No words can mend us!
Now that you know I'm not blind,
Considered a crime,
My soul under arrest,
My essence serving time!

But thank God for the light,

For now, I see

The reality that my mind didn't want to face.

Forgive Me...

Forgive me for hurting you, because of my past...

Angry at long lost liars... burning you like fire with my eyes!

Scorching you with cruel words, because of harmful untruths,

that had nothing to do with you!

Yet, you Love me, yet you hold me through the stones I've thrown!

Yes, forgive me, for now I'm grown!

A Felon's Prayer

Was I an idiot
Or made a foolish mistake?
Perhaps, a victim of my surroundings
And couldn't get a break.
Whatever the case,
It resounds in my face.
No lawful employment,
No mercy or grace.
No one owes me a handout,
But a hand up would be helpful.
Some choices I've made
Are deeper than the grave.
But how long must I pay
For my felony mistake?
No one hears my voice
Nor gives my talent or education a choice.
Fill out the application,
Listing the decisions of my past.
Upfront and honest;
Still treated so crass.

Denied with a smile
Or the sympathetic,
Let's just wait a while!
Judged constantly
On the systematic black and white.
Discussing this amongst my peers,
But we don't know who to fight.
Who will give us a chance?
Who will listen to the strength in our cries?
If God hadn't made me stronger,
I'd say goodbye…
Goodbye to positive change…
Goodbye to the new me
Living honest and free!
But, am I truly free?
When past actions haunt me?
Maybe, you can't understand;
Maybe you've never broken the law?
Or, maybe you have,
And you've never been caught!
Standing trial once,
But it's like we're living in court!
If I were a weaker vessel,
My soul would be dead.

Tossing and turning,
Dry bones in my bed!
But through it all,
I realize we're special…
God's love fills our head…
And when the pain cuts like a knife,
We'll still do what's right!
But instead
Of a weeping story,
We will shout until our voices are heard…
What used to rack my mind
Will be recorded in time
To the powers that be,
To those in earthly control.
I am but one person
Who represent a many of souls!
Souls that are smart;
Souls with a heart!
Souls that deserve
To make a fresh start!

Souls who aren't idiots;
Simply made a mistake…
And for the sake of humanity…
Our souls merit a break!

Never Be In Love With Lies

Something tells me…
deep inside…
you're not faithful…
so, no more lies…

Ever love someone's lies
and the way they made you feel?
It's amazing how deceit
can feel so real.

Some lies have a way
of making bitter taste sweet.
A persuasive touch
that makes the strongest feel weak.

You had an emotional hold on me.
Well, my low self-esteem gave you the grip.

Ever had to admit
that you were in love with their lies?
Ever wanted to believe they loved you?
Then, you finally found your nose
and saw the forest for the trees.

Been there, my friend,
but now, it feels good loving me.
It's time for us to stop searching for false acceptance
with our feelings on our sleeves.

There was a time
I resented you for the way you made me feel.
Then, I got honest with me.
I allowed myself to be a fish on your reel,
dangling helplessly
like a worm in the sea.

When all I had to do
was take some time and learn to love me.
Appreciate the God in me.

The survival in my fight,
the way I'm blessed to write,
the beauty in my sleep.

Instead of loving those lies,
let's respect ourselves
and who God molded us to be, inside.

Yes, I used to Love your lies, until I learned to Love me…
If you are still loving lies,
make the choice to love you more!

She is I, and I is She

She is I, and I is she… the woman who is
Destined to be…
So easily she inspires others,
Longing to see them aim higher!
She loves to see the growth
Of those who feel stagnated…
She loves to empower the powerless…
Feeding them words of life!
But so easily she denies her own right to shine…
Her right to grind!

She is I, and I is she… the woman who is
Destined to be…
Destined to have her God given voice heard…
A voice that used to be kicked to the curb!
A voice that will no longer be quiet…
She is coming out of the shadows!
If you've ever held yourself back…
Then, you know exactly what she means!

She doesn't desire to be seen…
For bragging rights… or the spotlight!
She wants to see more change…

She is I, and I is she…
The woman called and chosen by God…
Destined to be more than she ever felt she could be!
How do I know?
Because she is I, and I is she…

And if there's that beautiful, caged bird
Humming in your soul,
Go ahead and release her, Lovely.
You're never too old to live the life
That God and destiny has for you!

Is This You...
Lord Knows It Used to be Me...

She may spend the rest of her life alone,
Only because
She can't forgive
The ones who violated her trust.
She thinks suspiciously,
Even from the purest embrace.

IS THIS YOU?? PLEASE LET IT BE YOU NOW (NOW)

So, she depends on faith,
And forgets past snakes.
She forgives herself
And stupid mistakes.
She decides to Love,
Yes,
Even those that are fake...
The feeling is refreshing.

She chooses to live
With much Confidence,
Looking life straight in the eye…
Living her best life
By telling fear and hatred goodbye.

Don't Miss Out

Don't miss out on your smile,
because someone made you cry.
Don't miss out on the truth,
because someone fed you lies.
Don't miss out on peace,
because pain visited you.
Don't miss out on a friend,
because others have been un-true.
Don't miss out on your "Chance,"
because you WON'T forgive you.
Don't miss out on your life,
THERE IS MUCH MORE TO LIVE FOR…
Don't miss out!

For the Innocent Ones

For their innocent lives lost,
for their parents' pain,
damn the mad men
who are SICKLY insane.
For all the tears that've been shed,
the lethal lead,
their empty beds...
For any faith that was lost,
the blameless
that pay the cost...
God is with us all...
And my constant prayer...
Is that justice reigns...

Long Before We Were Born

Long before WE were created, God KNEW our plans!
And he holds them close, even if we don't understand!
Higher ground is near; have no fear!
Keep the Faith and your vision clear…
Because God has a Route planned especially for us
Long before we were born…

A Mother's Will to Fight

From the look in her eye
it's not hard to see
the Love she has for her children.

She is so real
about the troubles
she has faced.

Through wise counsel,
she is able to realize
what complicates her life
is artificial.

The conscience God gives her
represents her
positive outlook on life.

Therefore, her temporary setbacks
make room for her current triumph.

Forgiving...

You are nothing
like you portrayed yourself to be.
Loving arms, sweet nothings,
filled with worthless charm.
My heart was bitter,
saddened by your lies.
Blaming myself,
wondering why.
I couldn't see your deceitful disguise.
Forgiving you is so very hard to do...
but my wisdom knows it MUST be done.
When people hurt you,
they move on so easily with their life,
and the betrayed are left
trying to make things right.
We must choose to forgive,
being angry is too hard of a fight...
Choosing the key to freedom
which abides in forgiveness...

Don't Do That!

Baby, baby, baby don't compare yourself to my poetry!
She is my anchor,
a beautiful long lost story!
My pen has been with me
when I couldn't express my words.
Faithful by my side,
never telling a soul!
You are special,
the love of my life!
But asking me to choose,
you know that's not right!
My poetry is my passion;
we've been in love since I was twelve.
She is my outlet,
when I'm going through hell.
She's my friend when people wear many faces!
She permits me to go into those sensitive spaces.
Poetry and I have a timeless romance.
The words are the music,
and our rhythm is the dance!

I know it gets hard with me writing all the time.
But this is why
I'm always on your mind!
Poetry flows through the essence of my soul.
It allows me to warm your heart,
when you're confused and cold!
So, there is no competition;
no comparison between you and she.
Baby, baby, baby my poetry is the reason I am free!
She's the reason I am me!!!

Ever Had One of Them Days?

Ever had one of those days
Where nothing could help,
Not a smile, a laugh,
Or the strongest of prayers!
Yes, one of those days…
We all have them
At the oddest moment.
Even David, with his sheep
Wrote inspiring, sometimes sad poetry,
And like our brother, David,
This is a part of my story!
Thinking of loved ones,
Their bodies in graves!
Looking at these bills,
Watching the news,
All the senseless murders,
Enough to give you the blues!
Sadness that sends pain down your spine,
The deepest of agony,
That attacks the mind!

But instead of giving up,
A voice from within,
Says, "No need to worry,
For God is your friend!"
Then the words began to flow,
"You are Somebody,"
Look how you've grown!
You are more than a Conqueror;
This darkness must go!
You are not defeated,
But a warrior at heart!
And though you miss your family…
Many care for your heart!
So, allow peace to flow,
My eyes begin to see…
All isn't lost,
So, when depression attacks,
Remember God has our back!

Growth

Why are you are upset?
Is it because of my new found self-respect?
It's not that I don't Love you,
Oh yea,
I remember all the things we used to do!
We were some fools!
And had the nerve to think we were cool!
We were pretty cool, though…
Through the eyes of a fool.
Our life is worth more,
I said "OUR LIFE" not my life,
So, this doesn't mean goodbye!
Oh no, please don't cry.
Come with me;
No one should be left behind!
I just refuse to waste any more time!
We are not getting any younger,
Can't you hear the signs?
It's as Loud as thunder!!
Doesn't your mind ever wonder?

Wonder about change,

This scene is old,

Things can't remain the same.

Same old games, same old lies,

Oh… you don't want to go?

Then I must say goodbye!

Calm down,

No, I don't think I'm better than you!

Didn't you hear me say?

Damnit, I Love you!

BUT if you don't want to grow…

My friend I must go,

BUT if you change your mind… and you want to shine!

I'm a phone call away…

In search of better days!

My only prayer,

Is that you don't wait until it's too late!

BUT as for me and my Life,

We CANNOT wait…

Dear Poetry

Who would have ever thought?
You would connect so many hearts!
Amazing how God pre-destined you
To speak and reach,
To love, to share,
To meet and teach!
To be open and honest,
Clear and level,
Uplifting and inspiring
When that nasty devil of negativity
Attempts to hold us down.
You are lyrics of truth
With no ulterior motive.
Words that provide strength
And salute like soldiers!

Dear poetry,

You have many assignments Yet to fulfill,

When my pen may get nervous,

We must do God's will!

The will to love,

Leaving no soul behind…

And when I'm gone,

You will live throughout history!

Not for fame or glory,

But to lend a helping hand!

Spreading truthful stories

Of when I didn't understand!

Dearest poetry, 'til death do us part…

But even then,

You are forever my art!!

Sweet Nothings...

You can charm the red off a rose;
Finesse reeks from your bones.
Mmm, you put the S in Smooth,
But the real You
Sounds like a melody with no Key.
The old me adored the ground beneath your feet...
The true you smells like rotten milk,
While the new me, is free as mama's silk...
I gave you my voice
In the middle of our dance.
Lost in the wind
While needing a friend.
The new me now understands
And says to hell with you
And yo Sweet, wicked plan.
Sweet Nothings, a lesson very loud...
The new me isn't angry...
She is open like the range,
Loving the liberty,
Moving forward just the same!!

Dear Time...

Dear time never treated you like the lady you are!
Kicking it, loving it, wasting you hard...
But I have no regrets, learned from those lessons.
Grateful for every life learned blessing!
Another year to make it better...
Seconds leading to moments.

Dear time, dear time, I have learned to respect
The hands of your mind...
Catch ya in a minute... dear time, dear time!!

Sister Sister...

Called you sister...
Called you friend...
Never knowing
You were deadly to the end!
Gave you truth;
You fed me lies...
Such a soft face
With deceitful eyes…
But I'm not mad,
And I sure won't cry…
But for your safety,
I'm saying Goodbye!!

Holiday Blues

I miss them so much
The sound of their voice,
The warmth of their touch,
All the family commercials,
And seasonal cheer.
I smile open heartedly,
Still I yearn for you near,
But, I'll hold on to our memories,
As hazy as they are.
What I wouldn't give
To have you home for the holidays…
Signed, Holiday Blues…

In Memory of my family that have transitioned from this life…

Woman of the Night

She stands on the corner,
Flagging cars as they drive by.
Her eyes weighed down by mascara.
Her John picks her up in an old pickup truck.
She's repulsed by his smell,
But she has to put up.
Fifty dollars a shot,
Her life always in danger,
As well as her freedom.
This corner is hot.
She sees a police car
And pretends to talk on her phone.
Her body in place,
But her soul is at home!
She thinks back
About her younger days
And how she used to have fun.
Now, her life a huge saga.
This woman of the night,
Looked down on by society,

Wishing she had wings
To take flight.
The hour grows late;
Her world is so cold.
At times she thinks,
"Will I do this when I'm old?"
No retirement package, no 401-K,
Her means of survival-
To make it through the day.
She's had men of all types;
In three piece suits,
Basketball shorts,
Convicted felons,
And judges in court.
What can she do to get her life back?
Standing in high heels,
Her feet ache.
She smokes a cigarette;
The night comes to an end.
Plenty of money to spend,
Only problem is in her lifestyle;

She has no one to call friend.
She stands in the shower,
Attempting to wash away their touch.
She pours a drink,
Her insides want to yell,
Feeling like she's trapped in hell!
This woman of the night
Would give almost anything
To leave and take flight.

Fancy Fat

So, I've dressed you up, shined ya down
Hair perfect, nails polished, lipstick always flawless!
Aroma of sweet and fresh…
But is my blood pressure a high mess?
Car's clean, teeth on bling,
But what about my spinal scene?
Creative thoughts in place, mind on point,
But how are my knees and joints?
Business plan, friends understand,
Not worried 'bout fem or man!
But what's up with my healthy plan?
My Soul is Strong, and Spirit Glows…
But what about this extra weight I hold?
Made up my mind…
Not for looks, or physical appeal…
It's time I give my temple the respect it deserves…
No need in waiting until I'm old!
This excess weight has to go…
Cause you can dress it up… and shine it down!
But most importantly
We need good health to be around…

Breathe

I feel like my wings have been clipped,
like a captain who's lost his ship.

When do I get to fly?
Are all my days supposed to be immersed with cries?

How can I act like I'm strong?
Where on earth do I belong?

I don't want to sound weak, but my heart is split in two.
Been thinking all day,
and I don't know what to do.

Sometimes, all you can do
is think about your mistakes,
learn from your ignorance,
and allow your Breath to Breathe!

The County Jail I created for myself.

No Pain No Gain

…Crosses my mind…
The days in this life when I wanted to die!
The days when my heart believed
Every one of the devil's negative lies…
Lies of my existence having no worth!
Fueling suffered rejection and unnamable hurt…
Days that were dark… of a broken heart!
Days of remorse… days in court… days of sadness,
And THE nights were worse!
Depressing days… filled my space…
Days with only stolen food on my plate!
Days of searching for love on my back…
Days of rumors that I smoked crack!
Sinful Defamations from those I trusted…
Dedicated love for those who were only lustful.
Sweet nothing days… that filled my head…
The days I felt my Soul was dead!
Years of my own lies… refusing to cry…
Many nights, I begged God to Kiss me goodbye!
But oh Baby… THOSE DAYS ARE GONE.
Nothing is perfect,
But, at least now, I'm strong.

Now live the Moments of Peace so Strong!
Peace that has Purpose…
Love that is real… Choice Wordsss of Life…
That many Hearts can feel…
Days of forgiveness… of myself and others!
Futuristic compassion for my sisters and brothers!
Days where words no longer cut like a knife…
Days that my Reflection… Adored and reeked Light!!
So, if you've had one of those days…
Then, you know what I mean…
And if you still suffer silently…
I beg you to Breathe!
Release the guilt, the pain, the shame…
Love yourself… and God's Holy name…
Yes, those were the days…
My Spirit was enslaved…
And there is nothing worse…
Than being alive… and inhaling a grave!
Grateful for those moments…
They give much Appreciation to this Godly Freedom!!

Best Kind of Hatred

The best kind of hatred
is the type that makes us change!
Like missing The Sunshine,
settling for pain.
The kind of hatred
that prompts us to action…
It pushes us into our destiny
with peace, everlasting.
Best kind of hatred
removes fear from our eyes.
This kind of hatred
navigates us toward greatness
full of Wonder and surprise!
Hatred of not being whole,
mind, body, and soul!
The type of hatred that turns ignorance
into intelligent gold!
It allows us to forgive,
because we hate the bitterness regret holds.
It forces us to grow up,

losing the mentality of a child.
It raises that fast tailed girl,
changing her from being wild!
The hatred of mistakes,
like stealing from the plate.
The type of hatred
that gets sick of living simple
When we ARE born to be great!
Yes, the best type of hatred
is the kind that gives birth to Love!
It alters the thought
of that "ugly duckling,"
Allowing her to realize
she is a Beautiful Swan
who saves that lost little boy.
This hatred encourages single mothers
to go back to school.
And ignites a fire of revelation
to that law breaking fool.
Hatred of discrimination justifies an inner revolution.

The reason monumental souls
seek productive resolutions!
The type of hatred for bad knees
and painful steps.
It motivates us to stop over eating
and work up a sweat!
The type of hatred
for generational curses
makes real men the best fathers.
Teaching their seeds different,
so their offspring will prosper!
Yes, the best kind of hatred
invokes the sweetest love…
Maybe, there needs to be a little hatred inside of every one of us?

To the Poet in You

Here's to seeing the world through different eyes
as we look past the moment of "reality"?
Taking a chance,
speaking our voice,
no matter who understands.
To the expression of our souls…
The Vision we hold
For every time we pick up a pen
in our opinionated war,
we attempt to win
from our passion deep within…
In that moment, we strike a key,
revealing what we really feel!
To the author of creativity
who always keeps it real.
Continue to free your spirit
allow yourself to grow.
Whatever reason you write,
never give up the fight.
This is OUR Poetry, this is our LIFE!

Girl, I Heard

Girl, I heard,
Yes, I was a mess,
didn't know how to live FREE.
Some people thrive off of gossip.
They will sit and "listen" to your problems
as if they truly care.
But the fact is,
they may be present,
but their heart was never there.
A pair of lips can say any thing
at any given moment,
but the truth is
some people won't like you,
and that's okay.
What matters the most
is that you accept yourself.

I've learned
some people are lost
and very happy that way.
They long to see you floating on that same, miserable boat.
It makes them feel better
about who they may never become.
This gives them some twisted validation.
So, fly with the eagles
and tell THEM to keep what they've heard,
because you've finally learned how to live drama-free.

Her Story...

The same heart she adored
shattered her beat into a myth.
The same heart she loved
is a song she will miss.
However, it should never be heard, again.
Before the "love,"
they were friends...
But due to her Faith,
she'll never hate again...

Little Too Late

When I really needed you,
you weren't there!
Now you show up,
and for my own protection,
I can't allow my heart to care!
I'm not bitter.
I'm not sad, not upset, and I'm not mad.
You're a Little Too Late,
and that's a lot too bad!!

One Love

They judge him,
calling him a thug.
Never considering
he, too, needs love.
So, he's been in trouble
and had to see the judge.
This man is still someone's son.
He's learned from his mistakes
and still can't get a break...
Maybe, that's why his demeanor is so hard...
Before you judge,
know the story, honor human life,
for it is God's Glory…
Everyone has a different path.
What matters is how we choose
to move forward on our journey.

Special

We can't go back and change the things we've done,
But we can make better choices for new victories to be won.
Everyone is TRULY SPECIAL in their own way.
Love you more, starting today!
Spread that same Love, near and far.
Make someone's day a little less hard…
Much Love and Peace to every silent Star.
Know that you matter,
regardless of who you are.

All the Time

Can a Broken Heart
Imagine wounds of Love?
Yes...
Can a Depressed Soul Inspire...
She WAS I,
And I am no LONGER She...
Giving God the glory,
For this is all we Need!

How Long?

How long
must you pay for her mistakes?
How long
will you feed them love,
while they only envision a snake?
How long
will your arms of gentle
await the coldest embrace?
While they're afraid to come in,
because of painful history.

How long

do they require

for you to earn their trust?

How long

will you sail in fearful territory?

Before your patience becomes scarce?

Our life will be as healthy

as we allow it to be.

Reinvention

We Can, We Will, We Must…
Dreaming is a thought
past the subconscious.
Sometimes, nobody is on your bandwagon,
except you and your faith.
She may get lonely, but it's ok.
When faith gets weak,
fear will highjack awry
with no invitation.
This is when we demand courage to step up,
kicking fear out the door.
Then, our strength proudly tells fear,
you're not welcomed, anymore.
Faith reappears, belief is here.
Your vision develops,
your mission clear.

Lies will try to resurface
as doubt rears its ugly head.
Depression may knock at your door;
anxiety will increase.
Speak to your mind.
Send your soul a loud message!
Though life is complex,
you will not allow it to stress you.
We Can, We Will, We Must …
Because no matter what,
God has our back.

Sweet Kisses...

Been Kissed before... but never envisioned heaven's door!
Been touched many times... but never made my Core Shine!
Been held in the past... told it would last.
But this Kiss makes my River Flow!
The Kiss of all Kisses... A love throughout time...

Journey

Would you trade anything for your journey?

Would you change anything about your story?

No one can walk our path,

So don't you regret one tear.

Learn from past mistakes…

Every test makes us stronger,

So we press on

And shine a while longer… Amen!

Priceless

You are There when I'm down…
You love me when I'm sad…
You understand me when I'm frustrated…
You tell me the truth when I'm wrong…
You're not jealous when I'm winning…
I am BLESSED TO HAVE THE SIMPLICITY OF YOUR DIVINE…
Dedication… Peace... Strength and Love…
God, you are an awesome wonder!
Thank you for sending my baby, CK, my way!

Lil Girl Lil Girl

Lil girl Lil girl shaking yo aZZ, such a wasted shame…

Understand there is so much more to your beauty!

Your heart, your soul, surpasses the power of your booty!

I know the television implies it's just fine…

Only because they don't want you to utilize your mind!

Comfort zones prefer you as tasteless eye candy…

When you are the nectar in the center!

They want you to believe you have nothing else to offer

Than being half naked… pregnant in the projects coffin!

Sexy is all good, embracing your essence is a woman's right!

But you're barely out of puberty,

Already losing the fight!

Lil girl Lil girl… you come from Kings and Queens!

Your royalty isn't in diamonds and rings!

Your wealth is our history… chapters some want to remain a mystery!

Lil girl Lil girl…don't settle for scraps… twerking on your back!

You are a Beautiful Creation… full of strength and power…

Stop and recognize… Lil Girl Lil Girl…

Close your eyes and picture that…

You are worth more than living on your back…

Lil Girl PLEASE picture yourself living better than THAT!!

Love Zone

Thoughts of you… Such a Lovely Zone!

Only heard a whisper of your thoughts

Haunting chills... like the romance of Ghost...

Fantasizing of you holding me close!

Our connection is a stress free zone...

A zone where only truth and smiles are allowed...

Space where we are free like a spoiled child...

Moments that are cherished… and Graceful!

A Zone where I long to Caress your face…

Dedicated to those who find love, online. My love is at home, but to that lonely soul, Never give up! God knows what your future holds.

R&B

Rhythm and Blues… you are so darn cool!
You help people ease their mind…
Kick off their shoes and shake their behinds…
All in the name of rhythm and blues!
We make love to you, unwind with you, break up and make up to you!
R&B you will forever be… you are timeless
In the archives of our musical history!
You tell our story with sensual glory.
Rhythm and Blues… here's to your Melodic story!

Flowing

The top of my mind is back… all cares are left in the breeze!
The feeling I get when positive music flows within…
No matter what I'm feeling or the lack thereof…
A Good song elevates the Spirit and speaks to the Soul!

Blessing in Books

You are filled with history, lies, sadness and glory!
Many don't understand the power of a story…
You are overlooked, left behind on a shelf!
But those who are wise indulge in your wealth…
There are a number of experiences we embark upon!
It's up to us to research, separating lies from the truth!
The best books are those with no pictures…
Imagination is an awesome mystery!
I've neglected you at times…
For technologies allure… but you are simple…
A healthy way to kill time!
So, as for me and my house… I'll read until I'm blind…
But thanks to your wonder,
The soul will always see!

Love-Line

A Blood line doesn't necessarily mean there's a Love line…

Just because we share the same blood…

doesn't mean I owe you Love!

Call it selfish… but gone are the days

of you treating me like a scrub…

ALL IN THE NAME OF BLOOD…

Mhh… baby girl ain't such a baby, anymore…

and she isn't searching for acceptance at your front door!

Family is as family does…

and sometimes, it doesn't come from blood!

And that's okay, because love is love,

be it family, be it blood,

but I will always do my best to show real love!

Rain On

Your drops turn into puddles… then raise to a pond...
flowing with the lakes turning into Oceans!
Observing the clouds as they open and cry their nature out…
Amazing how you're a force so lethal…
yet you relax every facet of the mind!
I'm grateful for you and the flowers you bring…
If it weren't for you, there'd be no Spring!
You're nourishing and sexy,
romance is birthed in your presence.
You are heavy on a fresh hair due…
but we couldn't have earth without you!
Crops would die… and our land would dehydrate.
Please continue to shower us with your love… Rain on!

10 Words of Life

We have survived, now it's time to live some life.

I get sick of racism, but I refuse to hate.

Love is an action word, so here's to the movement.

I am my sister's keeper, because my sister is me.

Our heart is an organ; here's to people of action.

We are more than music, though the rhythm sings forever!

All isn't lost as long as we are TRULY found.

Quit asking permission and claim your rightful place of royalty.

Used to think you were "smart" until I educated myself.

You CAN'T even convince yourself, anymore; just stop playing games.

Sex is as sex does, but Making Love is Epic!

Grace and Mercy; they are our Friends, now new Journeys begin.

What used to make me mad ignites fuel for growth!

Our Heart is an Organ, Love is All about Action!

The essence of truth is everywhere; our choice to see.

Poetry is a release; it's better to write than to fight.

Remaining Positive is impossible dining with those who embrace Negativity.

A Woman Is

Wonderful, we are all unique!
Observant, our eyes are Always open!
Magnificent, we wear so Many hats!
Anything and Everything to Everyone!
Never sell yourself short; Our Heart & Soul are Priceless!!

In the Moment of Now

Ever look to your life and think DAMN…
WHAT THE HELL DID I DO WITH THE TIME?
Thinking too long can make you lose your mind…
Positivity is the place to be…
and most of my writings share stories of living free…
But today is one of those days…
one of those what's my purpose days?
Those days like…
is this talent going to ever get me paid days?
NOT THAT MONEY IS THE MISSION DAYS…
Always about the message days!
But some folks think "undiscovered" Authors are majestic slaves!
If you're not an author, you may not understand this pain…
BUT Never give up Kings & Queens of the Pen…
We MUST Keep the Faith, FOR our Victory is In…
In the moment of now…
In the moment of Now…
yes IN THE MOMENT OF NOW!!!

Power

If you're tired of the "noise" then become the voice…
tired of what you "see" then create a NEW station…
and if you don't think we have the power…
THINK AGAIN! Inspired by the "voice" of Change! All Good People…

Old Friend

Do you remember when we used to get lost in the music?
Talking about our favorite singers…
you would have thought we knew them, personally.
This is dedicated to you, old friend.
You were the first friend I called cousin…
I had to have someone to call cousin,
and you got it.
Oh, oh, oh remember Fred and Jane?
They lived on the balcony.
Two of my then feathered friends…
And even though they were two of the 1,000's in the air.
You fed Jane her wheat bread
and Fred his white bread with me, every morning
when you would spend the night.
Ahh, the freedom of a child's mind!
Though I was sometimes depressed,
your presence always made me feel safe.

Yes, you were that friend;
That friend that never made me feel bad about being fat.
The friend who understood
every bit of my weirdness
and my beautiful strange.
In a world of childhood cruelness,
your kindness kept me sane.
It's amazing how the road of choices
set us worlds apart!
But always know, old friend,
you have remained in my thoughts, prayers, and heart.
I used to be hurt and angry
that you chose to ex me out of your life.
But the grown woman now knows…
You were in no way on any type of street life…
and baby, I got so lost for a while.
Smoking weed…hanging out
no dreams…no aspirations no self-love, whatsoever…

but old friend, how things have changed.
I began to hang out with crowds I knew nothing about…
all in the name of needing a place on this earth to belong!
But oh, friend, how things have changed.
From what I've heard,
life's been pretty good for you!
So happy to know that you choose to live your life
and not simply exist.
So many monumental moments have taken place…
you found your wife, and I'm in love.
You've been Blessed to see flesh of your flesh
and blood of your blood.
We may have ended up on different sides of the tracks.
But if you need me, your friend is here,
no questions, no hesitations, I have your back.
Old friend, old friend, my sweet innocent childhood friend…
Hope life is still treating you kind.
Old friend, old friend, woke up this morning with you on my mind!

Morning Sun

This is the type of pain that can easily rock your mind.

It oozes down your chest, sending chills through your spine.

The kind of pain that any depressed heart can feel.

Now, if you've never been depressed

you can't comprehend this real.

This pain blocks sight of the brightest of rays.

It changes perception of the clearest of days.

But I know someone who can change the sound of hurt.

God can brighten this sickness

and clean up all that dirt.

He can heal those wounds that time and separation never did.

God can make the loneliness disappear.

How do I know… because it ate me alive for years!

You can have life and not simply exist.

Yes, I know this pain; it plagued me for years.

It drained my laughter, replacing it with tears.

No matter who loved me, fear would not allow them near.

But what I've come to know is a man of Love.

A man who truly understands your pain,

he sees every aching moment.

And Loves us past the brink of devastation.

So, there is light at the end of the rainbow.

And it's there for all to see…Baby the silver is clearly lined.

That pain can go away;

please, don't carry it another day!

Doesn't matter how strong you think you are.

Our God will wrap you in his arms!

His Love will keep you safe from harm…

Especially from harming yourself…

Now, you can wake up and open the curtains.

Let the morning greet you with her Beautiful Sun.

Make genuine connections.

And depend on those who need you.
Yes, you can smile from the inside out!
Instead of merely speaking happy words,
you can command peace from your mouth.
Yes, there is life past depression and oppression.
Welcome to the morning sun!

Happy Doctor King Day!!

Kind Words… Strong Soul AS Freedom Rings!
If only you knew the Deserved Honor…
Nothing like a Soul with Kingdom Purpose!
Gone in Body, but your DREAM lives on in Many!!
THANK YOU, Dr. King…

If the "hypocritical" Shoe Fits...

Preacher Man, Preacher man,
how much blood is on your hand?
Many of you are more corrupt
than any "THUG" in this land!
Souls are seeking,
hearts are Leaking,
because of your deceit…
Now, their faith is weakened!
You call me a sinner, but
My motives are pure.
Now you, preacher man,
I just ain't sure…
I think we'll both be surprised
when faced with Heavens door…
Preacher man, preacher man,
how much blood is on your hand?

For Our Mommies

Poetic Love to ALL Motherless People…

They may be gone in body, but they're with us in Spirit…

I see your eyes as I look in the mirror!

My heart aches… as my hand longs for your touch.

Time can move so fast!

To our Mothers Resting…

They're Never forgotten as long as our Hearts Beat!!!

A Sinner's Blues

I didn't mean to beat my wife;
I just lost control.

Didn't want to sleep around;
I know AIDS is on the rise,
but he was so sexy;
those lips, those eyes.

Why would I rob a bank
when I know there's a chance that I could die?

Why would I kill my baby,
because of the noise from his cries?

What would make me drink,
then think I can drive?
I see the commercials all the time,
and even know people that have died.

Why did I put a gun in my mouth- pull the trigger?
Overdose on pills,
jump out of a building,
even though I'm making millions?

Why am I searching for help on every leather couch around?
Hundreds of thousands of dollars an hour,
and still leave confused, and bound.

Why does my teenage son dress in all black,
praising the devil
with demons on his back?

Why does my daughter feel so unpretty
when she is as gorgeous as any model
that's making top dollar?

Why am I married to the man of my dreams;
successful, handsome,
and I still choose to use methamphetamines?

Why would I sell drugs in my community?
Aiding to the birth of crack babies?

Why would I pimp this hoe
when she used to be a lady?

Somebody, tell me,
does anybody hear me; my life is on the line?

Why do I continue to go against the system
when almost everyone I know is dead or serving time?

What makes me think that I'm not on drugs
because I only smoke weed?
I lie to myself;
I know it's laced with T.H.C.

Why do I hate you due to the color of your skin?
How could I want to see you dead,
along with your family and your friends?

Why am I twelve, addicted to sex?
I've tried everything by fourteen; only God knows what's next.

Could it be because no one is standing in the gap for me?
Are church folks too busy gossiping
and not praying for me?
Too busy arguing about the clothes they should wear,
while Satan seeks to devour mankind, everywhere.

I have put letters in the mail
So quickly, some take my money.
But when I need your prayers,
some of them are fake and phony.

I want to believe;
my spirit longs to be fulfilled,
but you got priests molesting boys,
preachers using women as toys.

This is just a note for all religious folks;
please, get it together.
Pray for me.
Don't talk about me.

We are dying out here;
just watch the news.
I am a sinner in distress,
and these are only some of my blues.
Thank you to the true Men and Women of God
who live by conviction and who are on a true Godly mission.

Baby Doll

Why hurt her when she loves you so?
Why hurt her
when you already know
all the hell she's been through
and she's only thirteen?
How dare you hurt her
when she's your family?
You share the same blood.

She's had to watch her back
since she was three.
No one to Love or take care of her.
No nurturing from her mother,
no protection from her father,
no tenderness from her brother.

So what does she do?
She finds false Love from an older lover.

She cried out for help,
but no one paid her any mind.
Then, when she says she's pregnant
you want to beat her behind.

Why are you shocked?
How dare you act surprised?
She yelled,
She screamed,
She kicked, she cried.

You told her to "shut up"
so you could hear your favorite song.

She needed you…
as a matter of fact, she needed anybody.
Her flag had a permanent place in the sky.

She was all alone out there,
and the world felt pretty cold.
She was only thirteen
and began to look old.

Now the state steps in.

She's trapped in the system
that can be a nasty, revolving door.
She's too old to be adopted and too young to be ignored.

She can't live on her own,
even though her experiences make her feel grown.

Her voice goes unheard
while looking for Love.
She found herself becoming a whore.

Baby doll is degraded at school,
passed from house to house
like a handy tool.

Don't think she doesn't know
that she's an income fix.

Now, do you understand?
Her head constantly aches
from her silent cries.

When she needed help,
you thought she was after attention.
Isn't it better now than the morning after?
A child is born.
then there's nothing much to do.
That's a part of the problem;
it's a cycle of abuse.

She needs Love
and a listening ear.
She doesn't require much.
Just show her that you care.

Brother... Brother!!

It's been many years since our paths have crossed!
I was saddened to see that in our time apart,
you got so lost!
What could have happened in your life to make you start smoking
crack?
I remember the days when we used to smile and joke...
You were my hommie, a brother, a friend!
You were always up to something, with YOUR sly kiddish grin...
I will never standing in judgment of you.
If you would have called me;
I would have gladly lended my ear to you...
Or been that listening ear.
You could have confided in me...
my shoulder would have caught your tears!
When our eyes connected,
your head lowered in shame!
The guilt of your choices
written on your face!

I asked you if had eaten,

you replied, "I'm alright."

No life in your voice,

no beam of light…

Whatever happens… Never give up!

You are worth so much more.

Brother, Brother, please do more with your life!

Incredible Love:

When you think of Love
always remember that pain has been endured!
But God and Destiny paved the way.
Now, Joy…Happiness and Love are even the More.
This Incredible Love
will lead these two hearts on new adventures…
They will hold one another…
cherishing the moments that life offers.
Incredible Love is that Love that doesn't remember the past
but appreciates the now!
Incredible Love is considerate and kind.
It embraces the body and makes love to the mind!
Incredible Love says,
No worries baby,
know that I got you!
Incredible Love understands
all their baby has been through!

It wipes away the tears,
appreciates the laughter!
Incredible Love is that moment of stability;
be it good… be it bad!
It's that Love that breaks down walls,
offering a supreme place of safety…
It sees through the madness,
speaking life, blocking out any negativity.
Even if no one else understands but the two hearts that are involved,
Incredible Love doesn't care.
It's the love that motivates the heart to carry on.
It's that strength in the midnight hour.
Yes, A Love so strong!
Incredible Love is just that…
It's incredible!
This kind of love is honest when it hurts.
It doesn't offer lies, but shares wisdom
to stimulate growth…
Incredible Love is a fortress when the world is cold.

This Love is priceless
and never grows old.
Incredible Love connected these two hearts,
so today, as you witness this holy matrimony,
pray that this love stands the test of time…
Pray that the Mr. and Mrs. BirdSong
forever whisper sweet melodies in one another's ear…
And when things get rough
and life happens,
God and faith
will CONTINUOUSLY hold them near.
Incredible Love is the reason we are here…
We SPEAK that Incredible Love…
Will lead and guide them
throughout many blissful years!
YES
Incredible Love is the reason we are here!

Dedicated to a childhood friend on her special day.

Mr. Ramsey

The days are long;
the nights seem longer without you around.

My mind often ponders,
remembering the days
we practically lived on the phone.
Long conversations
laughing about anything;
no matter the situation,
you would understand.

MY ANGEL WITH NO WINGS,
you were always there,
no matter what I needed.

As understanding as you were,
you would tell me the truth
whether it was popular, or not.

Thank you for a listening ear…
thank you for sound advice
and not laughing at my fears.

You were so young, with much wisdom,
yet liberal minded enough to enjoy your freedom.

They don't make um like you, anymore,
missing a real friend.

In memory of my Real gentleman of a Friend Curtis Ramsey

No More

In the back of my mind, I have to pretend that you are a miss.
I've created a space where honesty rules,
and your lies don't exist!
It's safer that way; not for me but for you.
Because now I'm grown, and I see through your games.
It's amazing how we make ourselves ignore the obvious.
We settle for pain and call it joy.
We accept less and smile as if
the world has been handed to us on a platinum platter
encrusted with diamond cut edges.
It's easier to fly those agonizing memories far far away,
burying them in the deepest place.
But now, I must move forward with my life,
because you deserve no more power.

No One is to Blame!

Perhaps no one is to blame…
the guilt and the shame!
The shame of having a Love so pure,
and we allowed our past to taint it.
Maybe, because we both have been so broken,
did the thought of Real Love terrify us?
But don't we deserve it,
regardless to what people said
or how they felt!
When we were alone,
we knew our hearts were Real.
The silence of a Broken heart
opens the window to every perfect memory.
And in that moment, we lost it
and saying goodbye.
Yes, this makes the soul ache with blameless cries.

You thought I wanted to be free…
I thought you were sick of me!
Amazing how these images
became our darkest reality.
The feeling was sickening.
That life and the world feels like
there's a laugh at me sign
tacked on my back.
It feels like the one Heart that loved me
and I loved no longer thrived.
In the past, it's been so easy for me to move on,
that's why I know our connection is special.
We are the fantasy that fills my poetry.
The mirror
of an ageless artist and his treasures.
Our music sounds like a beautiful melody that never ends.
However, through this horrendous pain,
our eyes never died.

Looking out the window,
to the naked eye, the sun shines.
But to a withering heart and mind,
thunderstorms arise!
Never thought the day would come
when I would awake
not looking into your eyes.
I hurt you, and you hurt me,
but never before has the pain wanted to leave.
You thought I didn't care,
but no matter where I went,
I carried you there.
I am sorry for becoming your nightmare,
when all I long to do is fulfill your needs.
Never thought of a life after ours!
But even if it's not with me,
I pray you don't miss...
Miss the passion we once lived,
the romance that was so blessed.

The second our lips connected,

no time was missed.

You tell me to Love again.

When it feels like our story

was meant to be forever.

It aches my mind

that you were out in the cold.

One day, I hope you understand,

that was never my plan.

I reached, and reached,

but you declined your hand.

My plan was to care for you

like you had given many others.

I respect you

way past the lust of being lovers.

Where's the Good in goodbye,

will the agony ever leave…

Or will I forever feel sorrow?

I guess no one is to blame…
for the guilt and the shame…
Maybe in the next lifetime,
we will feel a Love the same!

She Lives, She Breathes, She Grows

She wakes up yet another day;
body parts are swollen.
She reaches for the telephone to call her relatives
only to hear the words,
"you silly child, how many times have we told you?"
Her skin is bruised,
her spirit's used!
She settles for the mentality
that she must be born to lose…
Her mind reflects to past days of respect
when she earned her own money,
writing her own checks.
Before she knew it,
she accepted a life of less.
She never knew her soul's net worth.
She ignored the key sighs and agreed with the hurt.

It enveloped her mind; she feels suspended in time.
She wonders,
"will my life be this way until the end of my time?"
She walks toward the kitchen
to prepare his meal,
feeding him energy
that gives him the will…
the will to control,
the will to murder her one day at a time.
He rolls over,
never utters a word.
He thinks of her as his property.
A piece of clothing
that he chooses to wear throughout their lifetime.
She contemplates suicide,
"it must be better than living a lie."
Similar to the caged bird,
she too longs to fly.

She longs to inhale
just one breath of fresh air;
air that is free.
She lives, she breathes, she knows!
Then,
a light bulb flashes in her thoughts.
A moment of clarity visits her.
No one will come save me.
I'm not in need of life's charity.
I own the power;
the strength to walk away.
I have the courage to make decisions,
to choose a better way.
This road that I'm on
does not have to belong to me!
And the air I desire
has been here all along.
It is up to me
to be empowered and strong.

She lives, she breathes, she knows…
I made myself his prey
at the end of the day.
I allow myself to be his victim!
I am better than this abuse.
I'm more important than this cruelty.
She lives, she breathes, she grows…
He is not to blame.
I give him this awful power.
He's like a ship with no sail,
and my pity gives him the wind.
But this day is over:
I will not be victimized by my own sin.
She leaves, she breathes,
and the feeling is like a high.
Amazing, she thinks,
amazing am I!
Grand like the Opry-
rich like oil.

I'm Strong as an oak tree,
heavenly as the earth.
I'm Pretty as an Angel,
damaged like the rain forest,
yet I'm still here to grow.
I'm Still here to know,
still here to grow, still here to know,
know that I am worth so much more!
She lives, she breathes, she grew…
AND SHE LEFT!

Jealousy!

How can you hate me and envy my dreams?
How can you listen
and not know what they mean?
You were my diary,
second to my written words.
Now, you are angry,
because my pen is being heard!
No one comes before you,
except God Almighty!
Even when I saw controlling behavior,
I turned a deaf ear and created a blind eye.
In the moment of my strength,
your aura made me weak.
Perhaps, I loved you too much,
losing sight of my purpose.
Subconsciously, I knew,
but in my heart, you were worth it!

How can you hate the same one you "Love?"
Why is resentment
such a hidden glove?
Every move I made
was in the name of you and I!
So, maybe that's the reason,
Maybe, I slowly told God goodbye?
I'll see you later, Lord,
but right now, a sista's in "Love."
Forgetting one of his cardinal rules…
and that's place no one above Him.
When we met, I was lost,
but understand, I'm grown,
and God is the real Boss!
The Boss of my destiny…
The Boss of my life…
if I turn my will over!

Sweet heart, I'll miss you,
but you being jealous
was not discussed in this picture.
In my mind, it was different;
clear as a Bell.
But the naked eyes don't know
that I'm living in hell!
So, farewell to our season;
you already know the reason.
This cycle can't continue.
I must be about God's venue…
Just wish I would have known
that you had so much jealousy in you!!!

Cancer

Tomorrow isn't guaranteed!
I'll never forget the day we got the news!
Automatic shutdown, anger, and denial went into full affect.
Not this demon, again; anything but this…
It truly has no face, no color, shape, size or gender.
This demon doesn't care who it attacks.
And if diagnosed, you're blessed if it doesn't hand you a death sentence.
I've witnessed cancer put some of the strongest people on their back.
It doesn't matter how much money or how prestigious you are.

Cancer just doesn't care!!
Some treatment can make you lose weight or lose your hair.
This non-loving, un-caring, selfish, narcissistic self-absorbed beast
has the potential to catch any soul at any given moment.
Many families suffer, filled with questions.
Why did this goddamn cancer have to choose the one I Love?

It's like an infestation of cruel, bitter lies.
And when you think it's gone,
it can rear its unwelcomed head, again.
It feels like a knife is in your spine;
each turn is the look from the doctors
who have absolutely no idea of what to do?
Watching those you love suffer is a terrible pain.
Helpless and Hopeless are two emotions that I remember.
But God can help us fight the anger,
deal with the depression, and help us hold on to faith!
Cancer turns some warriors into fearful beings.

You and your tragic side effects can go straight to hell.
Instead of being filled with oppression,
let's choose to spread as much life that this life can offer.
Let's love the one we're with, regardless of this evil presence.
Let's make as many Happy Positive memories as possible…

Let's enjoy and appreciate each sunset,

as we understand the next one isn't promised.

Maybe take the scenic route for an ordinary trip to the store!

Visiting the beautiful botanical gardens worked for us!

Inhale the freshest air possible.

And any ignorance that passes your way…

Give it no energy!

Because we realize tomorrow just isn't guaranteed!!

In Loving Strong Memory of
Sylvia Victoria Cook
Frank Cook
Victoria Bernice Brown
Lois Curtis
James Smith
Mother Majors
And the ongoing battle for ***Carlena K.***

David

If you only knew the tears behind that smile,
the pain behind the poetry,
and the strength behind the struggle…

Inspiring Quotes from the Author

"Sometimes we look at our lives… and think I could be doing so much more! But the older I get I realize it's not about what we "could" be doing it's about what we have done… and what we will be doing."

5) Reflection is healthy, regret is useless…
4) Never let anyone or their ignorance become YOUR REALITY...
3) Never be your own worst road block…
2) God gives us the tools we need; it's up to us to build WHAT WE WANT…
1) Anything is Possible, when we realize, God is first…

CLAIM IT…

Favor is:

Anything we Need, God's got us.

Victory isn't easy or cheap, but it can be

OURS!

Regardless to the outcome, we don't have to fight Alone!

- Fear can Hinder Freedom.
- but Freedom Is Stronger than Fear.
- Higher ground is near, so hold on!
- Keep the Faith and your vision clear.
- Good and bad times are a part of Life!

APPRECIATE IT:

BE THANKFUL FOR those that mistreat you…

IT BUILDS STRENGTH AND CHARACTER!

BE THANKFUL for rejection… it makes us accept ourselves.

Thank OTHERS for THEIR doubt, it builds our faith.

Thank them for the hate, it increases our Love.

So Thankful for the lessons, one less we have to Learn.

- Opportunity is what we make it!
- Never Give anyone your Power or Dignity!
- Never give up on your dreams!
- Always believe in You!

"If they took your kindness for Weakness,
make them Accept your Strength for what it is..."

- We all have the God given gift of Choice.
- Take ownership of your persuasive Voice.

"We don't need validation…

but positive enlightenment is always healthy…

and constructive criticism is needed much".

- Common sense is highly under-rated!
- Nobody can do anything alone… but be Alone.
- Love you some you and spread that same love!
- We all have many faces, because life has many chapters!
- Keep it real with yourself; the mirror knows the truth
- Her strength is untold; her mask tells the true story!
- Today she unveils what her friends have known for years.
- She accepts the good and the bad, and doesn't hide.

Why I Write

I write because it's a gift

God placed within.

In a premier reality,

I RELEASE therapy through my pen!

It comes like second nature,

the messages God gives me,

then translates them via my pen.

As long as I can remember,

ink and paper have been my friends.

They are sacred and confidential

like innermost thoughts

held deep within.

I write to send Love

to release

words from our father

that are honest, and filled with peace.

Words of encouragement

Sometimes, woes of my life,

different heartaches and struggles,

sharing my story

of how God made it right.

Why do I write?

It's one of the things

I was born to do.

There's nothing more fulfilling

than walking in your destiny,

knowing the Lord is living inside you.

My name is Lydia "Born-to-Write" Cook.

And this is why I write!

~Sincerely,
Lydia BornToWrite Cook

Biography

Lydia is originally from Ohio. She is a compelling and versatile poet and playwright. Her short stories, breathtaking song lyrics, and inspirational spoken words flow from the deepest part of her soul.

Lydia's biggest passions are young people and women who are starting over, and her mission is to encourage and empower her readers and listeners to know that with God, faith, and confidence, anything in life is possible.

She shares painful truths from her life's journey, so they may be a beacon of light and hope. She is a firm believer that with divine timing, positive influences, and a change of our thought process, second *chances can take flight.*

   She has written two books to date, *"From Pain to Power"* and her latest feature, *"Blue Fire a Poetic Journey of our Emotions."* Her poetry is featured in *"Battered Shadows,"* a non-profit book of collective authors. It is dedicated to the NCADV (National Coalition against Domestic Violence), and all proceeds are donated to the organization.

Contact Info: choicewordsss@gmail.com
Visit our Blog at: http://choicewordsss.wordpress.com
FaceBook @ Lydia BorntoWrite Cook, and please, like our page at:
https://www.facebook.com/WrittenWordsssOfChoice

Acknowledgements

My Heart Thanks You...
My Soul Needs You...
My Mind Appreciates You!!

God, I thank you for every Gift and Talent!

Scribing is not only a gift from God, but it is one of the principal reasons oxygen continues to flow through my blood!

To my Mommy... I only had you seven years on this earth. However, seven years was enough for me to feel your love, respect your hard work, and admire your dedication to whomever and whatever you placed on the forefront of your soul and mind.

To my Daddy... you taught me boldness giving me key tools of survival that only a father can give.

To my one of a kind Warrior, Vickie! I wish you were here to see your baby sis all grown up. And if you can see and hear past the sky, I know you have your chest upright with pride! I love you and miss you!

D.M. You are a Strong, Intelligent Queen of a woman and the epitome of a Soul-Survivor! Your tenderness and strength go hand in hand, like a perfect marriage. I wouldn't trade you for anything! Love ya, Lady!

To my big brother M.J.B... you are a jack of all trades and a master of many! No matter what phase of life you are in, you are always a gentleman!! I love you, baby...

C.K. I'm grateful for every moment that we listen to one another and provide judgment-free zones of "unconditional love" and support. May God and his hands of time continue to bless and cherish our lives and space. I've never experienced a Love like ours ever!

Lois Curtis... The laughs, tears, and precious memories from 1240 are forever engrained in my spirit and mind!

To Maxine Brooks... I'll always love you for your unconditional *friendship and genuine support...My Spiritual Mother... my Best Sister Friend... and loving Cousin.*

Aunt Deborah, you always spoke love and life to me. Thank you, and I can't wait to send you on a much-deserved vacation!

Sylvia, you're a strong woman, and even in your cussing and fussing, love was your motive. I love you, Syl.

TyShawn, I'll never forget you, baby; I love my big cuz'.

Mon, 'my' Val and Era-Lee... You are three of the BEST FRIENDS, ever! You Ladies are more than my friends... You are my Sisters, and I Love you Dearly!!

Belinda... You are a beautiful woman inside and out! You've been my friend and big sister! I Love you very much Belind-May'.

To Abduo and Fatou... and of course, my Princess Anta... Sir Malcolm... you guys inspired me to go back to school, and it is paying off.

To the classy and Godly Shirley Magee... You are the essence of excellence being unstoppable! My journey with you has taught me many life changing things. Loving you and supporting you always... near or far!

Selina M. Thank you for being a woman of your word and past the "business" factor. I am Proud to call you Friend.

To my poetic Brother, Brave Nate. Thank you for always listening and sharing your blunt, realistic advice.

To every kind soul I've met on my journey, thus far, and because of past pain and rejection I sabotaged our connection... Your kindness will never be forgotten. Thank you to the brave Soul-Surviving woman I have become, who writes empowering and encouraging poetic words of life. And to that wounded child who provides me with "broken poetry" to help link other souls to their lane of freedom.

Last but so not least, Thank you to my loyal and supportive Facebook family!

~BTW~

www.ingramcontent.com/pod-product-compliance
Lightning Source LLC
Chambersburg PA
CBHW060017050426
42448CB00012B/2793